MW00948525

The Society of Mary is a devotional society dedicated to promoting devotion to Our Lady, the Blessed Virgin Mary in order to glorify her Divine Son, our Lord and Savior Jesus Christ. She is our patron under the title 'Help of Christians,' a phrase first used to describe her by S. John Chrysostom in the year 325 AD.

Our objectives are to love and honor Mary, to spread devotion to her in reparation for past neglect and misunderstanding, and to take Mary as a model in purity, personal relationships and family life.

It was our Lord Himself who gave us the command to honor our mother and our father. In venerating the Blessed Mother of our Lord, we love and honor someone he loves and honors, his own mother.

In the economy of salvation there can not be a single person more closely united to the Blessed Trinity than the Blessed Mother of our Lord and Savior Jesus Christ. Mary is the daughter of God the Father, the Spouse of God the Holy Spirit and the Mother of God the Son.

She says in the Gospel of Luke,

' For behold, from henceforth all generations shall call me blessed. For he that is mighty hath magnified me, and holy is his Name.'

What the Lord magnifies we too magnify, and holy is his Name.

Jesus Christ is truly our Brother and Savior and Lord. As he is our brother, we become adopted sons and daughters of God the Father. Adopted by our Father God, we also become sons and daughters of Christ's mother Mary. Jesus is truly our Brother by the ineffable grace of God, and Mary is just as truly our mother by that same grace.

Being members of Christ's body, the Church, we recognize his mother as our own; as the Mother of Jesus Christ, Mary is surely the mother of all Christians.

For more information or to contact us, please go to

www.SOMAmerica.org

or write to

**The Society of Mary
POB 930
Lorton, VA 22079-2930**

Meditation on the mysteries of our Lord's life in the rosary imparts grace, is a powerful armor against hell, destroys vice, delivers from sin and dispels heresy. It makes virtue and good works flourish, obtains abundant mercies, draws the heart from the love of the world and its vanities and lifts us up to desire eternal things; sinners are converted and the just persevere in grace to the attainment of eternal life.

The Anglican Rosary is a simple aid to meditation that helps us focus on the mysteries of our Lord's life, death, resurrection and ascension. In the rosary we occupy our hands and quiet our minds to better appreciate the wonders of our redemption, ask for the gifts of divine grace, and obey the command to "be still and know that I am God."

The first Christians of the East knew Jesus in a deeply personal way. They understood the healing, comforting power of the name of Jesus, and they built a simple prayer around this "Name that is above all other names," "the name by which we are saved." [Acts 4:12]

Since the Bible warns us against vain repetition in prayer, the important point in using the Jesus prayer is not the act of repetition itself, not how we sit or breathe, but to remember to whom we pray; and in this case the words are addressed clearly to our Savior Jesus, the Son of God and the Son of Mary.

The Rosary itself is a simple collection of beads strung with a cross, medal or other Christian emblem attached at the end of a loop. It is comprised of the cross or medal, one invitatory bead, four Lord's Prayer beads, called cruciform beads, and four groups of seven beads called "weeks."

The invitatatory bead represents our prayer for assistance and reminds us that we must always depend on God for every need, even our ability to pray. The four cruciform beads remind us to number our days, that we may gain a heart of wisdom: they remind us of the four points of the compass and that Jesus is the Lord of creation, they remind us of the gospels, the word of our faith; the four horsemen of the last days, and the seasons of our years.

The four sets of seven beads remind us of the seven days wherein the Lord created all things, the seasons of the Church year, and the seventh day, the holy Sabbath. There are thirty-three beads in all, one for each year of our Lord's life on earth.

As with most devotional tools, the Anglican Rosary may be adapted by the addition or subtraction of certain prayers in accordance with one's own inspiration. The following is a traditional form of praying the beads.

We begin by declaring and reinforcing our belief in the ancient creed of our faith. With the cross or medal we make the sign of the cross while saying:

In the name of the Father and of the Son and of the Holy Spirit. Amen.

And then we declare:

I believe in God the Father Almighty, Creator of heaven and earth, and in Jesus Christ His only Son, our Lord. Who was conceived by the power of the Holy Spirit, born of the Virgin Mary, suffered under Pontius Pilate, was crucified, died and was buried. He descended to the dead. On the third day He rose again. He ascended into heaven and is seated on the right hand of the Father. He will come again to judge the living and the dead. I believe in the Holy Spirit, the Holy Catholic Church, the communion of saints, the forgiveness of sins, the resurrection of the body, and the life everlasting. Amen.

Next, we pray on the invitatory bead the words of the Psalmist:

Let the words of my mouth and the meditation of my heart be acceptable in your sight O Lord, my strength and my redeemer.

Before the first cruciform bead we note to ourselves the mystery on which we intend to focus, then pray the Lord's Prayer on the bead, saying:

Our Father who art in heaven, hallowed be Thy name, Thy kingdom come, Thy will be done, on earth as it is in heaven. Give us this day our daily bread. Forgive us our trespasses as we forgive those who trespass against us. Lead us not into temptation, but deliver us from evil. For Thine is the kingdom and the power and the glory forever and ever.. Amen.

Then on each of the seven weeks beads we pray the Jesus Prayer:

Lord Jesus Christ, Son of God, have mercy on me, a sinner.

When we conclude the first set of weeks, we say:

Glory be to the Father, and to the Son, and to the Holy Spirit; as it was in the beginning, is now and ever shall be, world without end.. Amen

When we reach the next cruciform bead, we declare the next mystery, pray the Lord's Prayer, and begin again.

When we conclude the last of the four weeks beads, the rosary is complete and we finish by making the sign of the cross while praying the words of Saint Paul:

May the grace of our Lord Jesus Christ, the love of God, and the fellowship of the Holy Spirit remain with us all. Amen.

"Again I started off on my wanderings. But now I did not walk alone as before, filled with care. The invocation of the Name of Jesus gladdened my way. Everybody was kind to me. It was as though everyone loved me...If anyone harms me, I have only to think, "How sweet is the prayer of Jesus!" and the injury and the anger alike pass away and I forget it all."

From "The Way of the Pilgrim"

Hail Mary, full of grace, the Lord is with thee. Blessed art thou among women and blessed is the fruit of thy womb, Jesus. Holy Mary, Mother of God, pray for us sinners, now and at the hour of our death.

Amen.

"May God the Father who made me bless me. May God the Son send his healing to me. May God the Holy Spirit move within me, giving me eyes to see with, ears to hear with, and hands that His work might be done. May I walk and preach the word of God to all. May the angel of peace watch over me and lead me at last by God's grace to the Kingdom."

Amen.

O God, whose only-begotten Son, by his life, death and resurrection has purchased for us the rewards of eternal life; grant, I beseech Thee, that, meditating upon these mysteries of the most holy Rosary, I may imitate what they contain and obtain what they promise, through the same Christ our Lord.

Amen.

May the souls of the faithful departed, through the mercy of God, rest in peace.

Amen.

Favorite Mysteries

The Joyful [Monday & Saturday]
The Annunciation: Luke 1:26

The Nativity: Luke 2:1

The Presentation: Luke 2:22

Finding Jesus: Luke 2:46

The Luminous [Thursdays]
The Baptism: Matt. 3:17

The Wedding: John 2:11

The Transfiguration: Matt. 17:1

The Eucharist: Luke 22:14

The Sorrowful [Tuesday & Friday]
The Agony: Matt. 26:36

The Humiliation: Matt: 27:26-27

The Cross: John 19:17

The Crucifixion: Matt. 27:33

The Glorious [Wednesday & Sunday]
The Resurrection: Mark 16

The Ascension: Acts 1:9

Pentecost: Acts 2:1

The Crowning: Rev. 3:21

When we pray the rosary we have something to occupy our hands, our mouths, our ears and our eyes. The simplest way to begin using the rosary is to read the meditation that accompanies each mystery, and then to gaze at the picture while reciting the appropriate prayers.

As we coordinate our activity and begin to relax, we can imagine ourselves present at the extraordinary event on which we are focused. As we ask for the Lord's mercy, we are moved to awe and wonder at his power, graciousness and love. We come to better appreciate the depths and breadth of these wondrous events that can never be completely known or understood.

The rosary, like any form of meditation, is a discipline that must be practiced to be appreciated in its entirety. Find a quiet, comfortable spot and carve out a few minutes of your day for service to the Lord and his Church in prayer: If you're willing to put forth even this small effort and trust in your loving Savior Jesus, we promise that your efforts will be well rewarded.

What Child Is This
Written by William Chatterton Dix

What child is this who laid to rest
On Mary's lap is sleeping
Whom angels greet with anthems sweet
While shepherds watch are keeping

This, this is Christ the King
Whom shepherds guard and angels sing
Haste, haste to bring him laud
The babe, the son of Mary

Picture the scene of the Annunciation. God proposes the mystery of the Incarnation which He will accomplish in the Virgin Mary—but not until she has given her consent. At this moment Mary represents all of us in her own person; it is as if God is waiting for the response of the humanity to which He longs to unite Himself. What a solemn moment this is!

For upon this moment depends the decision of the most vital mystery of Christianity. Full of faith and confidence in the heavenly message and entirely submissive to the Divine Will, the Virgin Mary replies in a spirit of complete and absolute abandonment: "Behold the handmaid of the Lord; be it done to me according to Thy word." This "Fiat" is Mary's consent to the Divine Plan of Redemption.

It is like an echo of the "Fiat" of the creation of the world. But this is a new world, a world infinitely superior, a world of grace, which God will cause to arise in consequence of Mary's consent, for at that moment the Divine Word, the second Person of the Blessed Trinity, becomes Man in Mary: "And the Word was made Flesh and dwelt among us."

PRAY

Our Father...

Lord Jesus Christ...

After completing the seven weeks beads say,

Glory be to the Father...

Ask for the grace of Christian Charity and pray for the lives of the unborn.

PERSONAL REFLECTIONS:

The First Joyful Mystery

The Annunciation

In the sixth month, God sent the angel Gabriel to Nazareth, a town in Galilee, to a virgin pledged to be married to a man named Joseph, a descendant of David. The virgin's name was Mary. The angel went to her and said, "Greetings, you who are highly favored! The Lord is with you." Mary was greatly troubled at his words and wondered what kind of greeting this might be. But the angel said to her, "Do not be afraid, Mary, you have found favor with God. You will be with child and give birth to a son, and you are to give him the name Jesus. He will be great and will be called the Son of the Most High. The Lord God will give him the throne of his father David, and he will reign over the house of Jacob forever; his kingdom will never end." "How will this be," Mary asked the angel, "since I am a virgin?" The angel answered, "The Holy Spirit will come upon you, and the power of the Most High will overshadow you. So the holy one to be born will be called the Son of God. Even Elizabeth your relative is going to have a child in her old age, and she who was said to be barren is in her sixth month. For nothing is impossible with God." "I am the Lord's servant," Mary answered. "May it be to me as you have said." Then the angel left her.

The Virgin Mary sees in the Infant that she has given to the world, a child in appearance like all other children, the very Son of God. Mary's soul was filled with an immense faith which welled up in her and surpassed the faith of all the just men of the Old Testament; this is why she recognized her God in her own Son. This faith manifests itself externally by an act of adoration. She adored from the first, and so too do we adore the God-made-Man, our Lord and Savior Jesus. Think of it: The Creator of all worlds deigned to be born a helpless infant; The King of the Universe consents to be born in a stable; The Master of all things accepts subjection to his human mother and step-father. Called the Man of Sorrows by Isaiah, our Savior began his life in the most abject poverty and in sorrow. Scripture also tells us that all things work together for good to those who love God, and so we see the Angelic host making declaration to the Shepherds that they brought 'good tidings of great joy.' In this we see the great mystery that poverty of spirit produces the rich fruit of heavenly glory. Such humility allowed the Blessed Mother to look down at the child nursing at her breast and in the same moment adore her child and her God.

PRAY

Our Father…

Lord Jesus Christ…

After completing the seven weeks beads say,

Glory be to the Father…

Ask for confidence in God and grace for all children

PERSONAL REFLECTIONS:

The Second Joyful Mystery
The Nativity of our Lord

And there were shepherds living out in the fields nearby, keeping watch over their flocks at night. An angel of the Lord appeared to them, and the glory of the Lord shone around them, and they were terrified. But the angel said to them, "Do not be afraid. I bring you good news of great joy that will be for all the people. Today in the town of David a Savior has been born to you; he is Christ the Lord. This will be a sign to you: You will find a baby wrapped in cloths and lying in a manger." Suddenly a great company of the heavenly host appeared with the angel, praising God and saying, "Glory to God in the highest, and on earth peace to men on whom his favor rests." When the angels had left them and gone into heaven, the shepherds said to one another, "Let's go to Bethlehem and see this thing that has happened, which the Lord has told us about." So they hurried off and found Mary and Joseph, and the baby, who was lying in the manger. When they had seen him, they spread the word concerning what had been told them about this child, and all who heard it were amazed at what the shepherds said to them. But Mary treasured up all these things and pondered them in her heart.

On the day of the Presentation God received infinitely more glory than he had hitherto received in the temple from all the sacrifices and all the holocausts of the Old Testament. On this day it is his own Son Jesus who is offered to him, and who offers to the Father the infinite homage of adoration, thanksgiving, expiation and supplication. This is indeed a gift worthy of God. It is from the hands of the Virgin Mary and her husband Joseph that this offering, so pleasing to God, is received. For the first time the Lord God has entered his holy Temple, and for the first time our Jesus sheds his blood for us sinners. The Great King has entered his courts, and already it is to suffer and to bleed for our sakes, with his Mother looking on. This scene will be repeated thirty three years later at Calvary, and again his Blessed Mother will be there. Here she receives the prophesy that her child will be Salvation for all people, a light to lighten the Gentiles, and that a sword will pierce her own soul also. All Mary and Joseph could give were two doves or pigeons, the sacrificial offering reserved for the poorest of people. In the Nativity our Lord offered himself to the world in poverty, and in the Temple he offers himself to His Father the same way, just as he will again at the end of his earthly life.

PRAY

Our Father…

Lord Jesus Christ…

After completing the seven weeks beads say,

Glory be to the Father…

Ask for the gift of Moral Courage and grace for all families.

PERSONAL REFLECTIONS:

The Third Joyful Mystery

The Presentation

When the time of their purification according to the Law of Moses had been completed, Joseph and Mary took him to Jerusalem to present him to the Lord (as it is written in the Law of the Lord, "Every firstborn male is to be consecrated to the Lord"), and to offer a sacrifice in keeping with what is said in the Law of the Lord: "a pair of doves or two young pigeons." Now there was a man in Jerusalem called Simeon, who was righteous and devout. He was waiting for the consolation of Israel, and the Holy Spirit was upon him. It had been revealed to him by the Holy Spirit that he would not die before he had seen the Lord's Christ. Moved by the Spirit, he went into the temple courts. When the parents brought in the child Jesus to do for him what the custom of the Law required, Simeon took him in his arms and praised God, saying: "Sovereign Lord, as you have promised, you now dismiss your servant in peace. For my eyes have seen your salvation, which you have prepared in the sight of all people, a light for revelation to the Gentiles and for glory to your people Israel." The child's father and mother marveled at what was said about him.

"How is it that you sought me? Did you not know that I must be about My Father's business?" This is the answer that Jesus gave to his Mother when, after three days' search she had the joy of finding him in the Temple. These are the first words coming from the lips of the Word Incarnate to be recorded in the Gospel. In these words Jesus sums up his whole person, his whole life, his whole mission. Christ's whole life will only be a clarifying and magnificent exposition of the meaning of these words. Think too of the events leading up to this scene: Mary and Joseph, the two holy people chosen by the Father to guard his only Son, lost God. Not by wickedness or sin did they loose sight of the Lord, but by simple, plain, human inattention. They were traveling, they were preoccupied, and they were busy. So busy in fact that they lost not just their child, but they lost track of their own Lord and Savior as well. How truly this speaks to our human condition! They searched among their companions, they searched the places they had been, and when they finally found God, where was he? In Church, teaching his doctrine of grace and salvation. Does this not still surprise us as it surprised them? Where do we look when we have lost God?

PRAY

Our Father…

Lord Jesus Christ…

After completing the seven weeks beads say,

Glory be to the Father…

Ask for the gift of Godly Wisdom and pray for all elderly persons.

PERSONAL REFLECTIONS:

The Fourth Joyful Mystery

Finding Jesus

Every year his parents went to Jerusalem for the Feast of the Passover. When he was twelve years old, they went up to the Feast, according to the custom. After the Feast was over, while his parents were returning home, the boy Jesus stayed behind in Jerusalem, but they were unaware of it. Thinking he was in their company, they traveled on for a day. Then they began looking for him among their relatives and friends. When they did not find him, they went back to Jerusalem to look for him. After three days they found him in the temple courts, sitting among the teachers, listening to them and asking them questions. Everyone who heard him was amazed at his understanding and his answers. When his parents saw him, they were astonished. His mother said to him, "Son, why have you treated us like this? Your father and I have been anxiously searching for you." "Why were you searching for me?" he asked. "Didn't you know I had to be in my Father's house?" But they did not understand what he was saying to them.

John baptized with water, having said that Jesus would baptize with the Holy Spirit and with fire, a prophecy he later fulfilled at Pentecost. As Jesus comes out of the water, the Holy Spirit descends upon him like a dove, the heavens open and the Father's voice is heard from on high: "You are my beloved Son; with you I am well pleased" Thus the event of Christ's Baptism is not only a revelation of his divine Sonship, but at the same time a revelation of the whole Blessed Trinity. The Father's voice from on high reveals in Jesus the Only-Begotten Son and all this comes about by virtue of the Holy Spirit who, in the form of a dove descends on Christ, the Lord's Anointed. Obedient to the Father's will, our Lord consents to be baptized by John and is anointed by the Holy Spirit, commissioned to begin his public ministry and publicly proclaimed as the Only Begotten Son. He arose from the waters of the Jordan with the grace of God the Holy Spirit upon him, as he would later rise from the grave by that same Spirit. We too rise from the waters of our own baptism by the grace of the Spirit, washed from sin, infused with new life and empowered by God to participate in the life of that same Trinity; Father, Son and Holy Spirit.

PRAY

Our Father…

Lord Jesus Christ…

After completing the seven weeks beads say,

Glory be to the Father…

Ask for zeal for the glory of God and pray for all priests and religious.

PERSONAL REFLECTIONS:

The First Luminous Mystery

The Baptism

Then Jesus came from Galilee to the Jordan to be baptized by John. But John tried to deter him, saying, "I need to be baptized by you, and do you come to me?" Jesus replied, "Let it be so now; it is proper for us to do this to fulfill all righteousness." Then John consented. As soon as Jesus was baptized, he went up out of the water. At that moment heaven was opened, and he saw the Spirit of God descending like a dove and lighting on him. And a voice from heaven said, "This is my Son, whom I love; with him I am well pleased."

The Blessed Mother here presents her Divine Son with a problem. She doesn't tell him how to fix it or otherwise give advice, she simply trusts her son and Lord do whatever is best and instructs the servants, as she instructs us from the gospel to, "Do whatever he tells you." Our Lord on his part simply tells the servants to draw out water and take it to the steward, he doesn't offer a prayer or ask the Father for the grace of a miracle, instead he accomplishes it by an act of his own will. Only God can create and re-make his creation by a simple act of will, all other prophets and holy people have to depend on God to effect miraculous change. Not so our Lord. This public miracle not only blesses and sanctifies the state of holy matrimony, it inaugurates his public ministry. Today he changes water into wine, and tomorrow he will change wine into his own precious blood. His miracles give witness to his Godhood, announcing his power, proving his divinity and verifying his witness of himself and his Father. We have to be prepared for miracles, we can only grasp so much so fast. In initiating his public ministry with this one act, he begins to prepare us to accept the feeding of the thousands, the healing of the multitudes and finally, the sacrifice of his cross and the glories of his resurrection and ascension.

PRAY

Our Father…

Lord Jesus Christ…

After completing the seven weeks beads say,

Glory be to the Father…

Ask for increased faith and pray for the needs of your own family.

PERSONAL REFLECTIONS:

The Second Luminous Mystery

The Wedding at Cana

On the third day a wedding took place at Cana in Galilee. Jesus' mother was there, and Jesus and his disciples had also been invited to the wedding. When the wine was gone, Jesus' mother said to him, "They have no more wine." "Dear woman, why do you involve me?" Jesus replied, "My time has not yet come." His mother said to the servants, "Do whatever he tells you." Nearby stood six stone water jars, the kind used by the Jews for ceremonial washing, each holding from twenty to thirty gallons. Jesus said to the servants, "Fill the jars with water"; so they filled them to the brim. Then he told them, "Now draw some out and take it to the master of the banquet." They did so, and the master of the banquet tasted the water that had been turned into wine. He did not realize where it had come from, though the servants who had drawn the water knew. Then he called the bridegroom aside and said, "Everyone brings out the choice wine first and then the cheaper wine after the guests have had too much to drink; but you have saved the best till now." This, the first of his miraculous signs, Jesus performed in Cana of Galilee. He thus revealed his glory, and his disciples put their faith in him.

Here we see our Lord as the Psalmist did, as 'the fairest of the sons of men.' To be transfigured means to be transformed, changed, re-created into something wholly new and bright and glorious. We contemplate the Transfiguration of our Lord and anticipate the transfiguration of our selves as we are continually renewed and strengthened and converted by the Word of God and the grace of his Spirit. Whether awake in Christ or asleep in Christ, still we are all alive in Christ according to St. Paul. Here we see that doctrine expressed tangibly as Moses, representing the Law, and Elijah, representing the Prophets, are both shown conversing with our Lord. In the Communion of the Saints both Moses and Elijah are indeed alive in Christ. And our Lord in his turn sums up in his own Sacred Person both the Law and the Prophets. Like the Apostles we are confused, dazzled and overwhelmed with the glory and the depth of the event that confronts us. And like them we must process what we've been shown over the course of time, descending from the mountain top to the valley beneath to minister and share the work of the Lord as we progress on our journey, ever striving in that holy hope and confidence that one day we too shall be transformed.

PRAY

Our Father...

Lord Jesus Christ...

After completing the seven weeks beads say,

Glory be to the Father...

Ask for personal transformation and pray for the needs of your local Church.

PERSONAL REFLECTIONS:

The Third Luminous Mystery
The Transfiguration

After six days Jesus took with him Peter, James and John the brother of James, and led them up a high mountain by themselves. There he was transfigured before them. His face shone like the sun, and his clothes became as white as the light. Just then there appeared before them Moses and Elijah, talking with Jesus. Peter said to Jesus, "Lord, it is good for us to be here. If you wish, I will put up three shelters—one for you, one for Moses and one for Elijah." While he was still speaking, a bright cloud enveloped them, and a voice from the cloud said, "This is my Son, whom I love; with him I am well pleased. Listen to him!" When the disciples heard this, they fell facedown to the ground, terrified. But Jesus came and touched them. "Get up," he said. "Don't be afraid." When they looked up, they saw no one except Jesus.

Christ's death on the cross, the culmination of his whole life of obedience, was the one, perfect and sufficient sacrifice for the sins of the world. There can be no repetition of or addition to what was then accomplished once for all by Christ. The Eucharistic memorial is no mere calling to mind of a past event or of its significance, but the church's effectual proclamation of God's mighty acts. Communion with Christ in the Eucharist presupposes his true presence, effectually signified by the bread and wine which, in this mystery, become his body and blood. Thus, in considering the mystery of the Eucharistic presence, we must recognize both the sacramental sign of Christ's presence and the personal relationship between Christ and the believer which arises from that presence. The Lord's words at the last supper, "Take and eat; this is my body", do not allow us to dissociate the gift of the presence and the act of sacramental eating. The elements are not mere signs; Christ's body and blood become really present and are really given. But they are really present and given in order that, receiving them, believers may be united in communion with Christ the Lord. The Lord who thus comes to his people in the power of the Holy Spirit is the Lord of glory. In the Eucharistic celebration we anticipate the joys of the age to come. By the transforming action of the Spirit of God, earthly bread and wine become the heavenly manna and the new wine, the eschatological banquet for the new man: elements of the first creation become pledges and first fruits of the new heaven and the new earth.

PRAY

Our Father…

Lord Jesus Christ…

After completing the seven weeks beads say,

Glory be to the Father…

Ask for the gift of union with Christ and pray for the conversion of sinners.

PERSONAL REFLECTIONS:

The Fourth Luminous Mystery

The Eucharist

When the hour came, Jesus and his apostles reclined at the table. And he said to them, "I have eagerly desired to eat this Passover with you before I suffer. For I tell you, I will not eat it again until it finds fulfillment in the kingdom of God." After taking the cup, he gave thanks and said, "Take this and divide it among you. For I tell you I will not drink again of the fruit of the vine until the kingdom of God comes." And he took bread, gave thanks and broke it, and gave it to them, saying, "This is my body given for you; do this in remembrance of me." In the same way, after the supper he took the cup, saying, "This cup is the new covenant in my blood, which is poured out for you."

It is for the love of his Father above all else that Jesus willed to undergo his Passion. Behold Jesus Christ in his agony. For three long hours weariness, grief, fear and anguish sweep in upon his soul like a torrent; the pressure of this interior agony is so immense that blood bursts forth from his sacred veins. What an abyss of suffering is reached in this agony! And what does Jesus say to his Father? "Father, if it be possible, let this chalice pass from me." Can it be that Jesus no longer accepts the will of his Father? Certainly he does. But this prayer is the cry of poor human nature, crushed by ignominy and suffering. Now is Jesus truly a "Man of Sorrows." Our Savior feels the terrible weight of his agony bearing down upon his shoulders. He wants us to realize this; that is why he utters such a prayer. But listen to what he immediately adds: "Nevertheless, Father, not my will but Thine be done." Here is the triumph of love. Because he loves His Father, he places the will of his Father above everything else and accepts every possible suffering in order to redeem us. For this we pray in the rosary, "Lord Jesus Christ, son of God, have mercy on me, a sinner."

PRAY

Our Father…

Lord Jesus Christ…

After completing the seven weeks beads say,

Glory be to the Father…

Ask for the gift of Piety and pray for the relief of the poor.

PERSONAL REFLECTIONS:

The First Sorrowful Mystery

The Agony

Then Jesus went with his disciples to a place called Gethsemane, and he said to them, "Sit here while I go over there and pray." He took Peter and the two sons of Zebedee along with him, and he began to be sorrowful and troubled. Then he said to them, "My soul is overwhelmed with sorrow to the point of death. Stay here and keep watch with me." Going a little farther, he fell with his face to the ground and prayed, "My Father, if it is possible, may this cup be taken from me. Yet not as I will, but as you will." Then he returned to his disciples and found them sleeping. "Could you men not keep watch with me for one hour?" he asked Peter. "Watch and pray so that you will not fall into temptation. The spirit is willing, but the body is weak." He went away a second time and prayed, "My Father, if it is not possible for this cup to be taken away unless I drink it, may your will be done." When he came back, he again found them sleeping, because their eyes were heavy. So he left them and went away once more and prayed the third time, saying the same thing.

Christ substituted Himself voluntarily for us as a sacrificial victim without blemish in order to pay our debt, and, by the expiation and the satisfaction which He made for us, to restore the Divine life to us. This was the mission which Christ came to fulfill, the course which He had to run. Christ Jesus becomes an object of derision and insults at the hands of the temple servants. Behold Him, the all-powerful God, struck by sharp blows; His adorable face, the joy of the saints, is covered with spittle; a crown of thorns is forced down upon the head of the King of all Creation; a purple robe of royalty is placed upon his shoulders as a mock of derision; a reed is thrust into his hand to imitate a scepter; the servants genuflect insolently before Him in mockery. What an abyss of ignominy! What humiliation and disgrace for One before whom the angels tremble! The cowardly Roman governor imagines that the hatred of the Jews will be satisfied by the sight of Christ in this pitiful state. He shows him to the crowd: "Ecce Homo—Behold the Man!" Let us contemplate our Divine Master at this moment, plunged into the abyss of suffering and ignominy, and let us realize that the Father also presents Him to us and says to us: "Behold My Son, the splendor of My glory—but bruised for the sins of My people."

PRAY

Our Father…

Lord Jesus Christ…

After completing the seven weeks beads say,

Glory be to the Father…

Ask for the gift of humility and pray for those who suffer for the faith.

PERSONAL REFLECTIONS:

The Second Sorrowful Mystery

The Humiliation of our Lord

Then the governor's soldiers took Jesus into the Praetorium and gathered the whole company of soldiers around him. They stripped him and put a scarlet robe on him, and then twisted together a crown of thorns and set it on his head. They put a staff in his right hand and knelt in front of him and mocked him. "Hail, king of the Jews!" they said. They spit on him, and took the staff and struck him on the head again and again. After they had mocked him, they took off the robe and put his own clothes on him. Then they led him away to crucify him.

Let us meditate upon Jesus Christ on the way to Calvary laden with His cross. He falls under the weight of this burden. To expiate sin, He wills to experience in His own flesh the oppression of sin. Fearing that Jesus will not reach the place of crucifixion alive, the Jews force Simon of Cyrene to help Christ to carry His cross, and Jesus accepts this assistance.

In this Simon represents all of us. As members of the Mystical Body of Christ, we should all help Jesus to carry His Cross. This is the one sure sign that we belong to Christ—if we carry our cross with Him. But while Jesus carried His cross, He merited for us the strength to bear our trials with generosity. He has placed in His cross a sweetness which makes ours bearable, for when we carry our cross it is really His that we receive. For Christ unites with His own the sufferings, sorrows, pains and burdens which we accept with love from His hand, and by this union He gives them an inestimable value, and they become a source of great grace for us.

It is above all His love for His Father which impels Christ to accept the sufferings of His Passion, but it is also the love which He bears us.

PRAY

Our Father...

Lord Jesus Christ...

After completing the seven weeks beads say,

Glory be to the Father...

Ask for the gift of self-mortification and pray for the sick.

PERSONAL REFLECTIONS:

The Third Sorrowful Mystery

The Cross

Carrying his own cross, he went out to the place of the Skull (which in Aramaic is called Golgotha).

At the Last Supper, when the hour had come to complete His oblation of self, what did Christ say to His Apostles who were gathered around Him? "Greater love than this no man hath, that a man lay down his life for his friends." And this is the love, surpassing all loves, which Jesus shows us. What greater proof of love could He have given us? None. Hence the Apostle declares without ceasing that "because He loved us, Christ delivered Himself up for us." Delivered even to death on a cross! "He offered Himself because He willed it." These words tell us how spontaneously Jesus accepted His Passion. This freedom with which Jesus delivered Himself up to death for us is one of the aspects of His sacrifice which touch our human hearts most profoundly. We cannot help but be moved by compassion for the Blessed Mother, standing at the foot of a cross which was covered in her child's Most Precious Blood, watching him die alone, abused and abandoned. The Father did not sacrifice himself; instead he sacrificed something more precious to any parent, his only, true and adorable Son. In accepting the Father's will and standing at the foot of the cross Mary also made that sacrifice and gave up her only beloved Son, that we might be redeemed.

PRAY

Our Father…

Lord Jesus Christ…

After completing the seven weeks beads say,

Glory be to the Father…

Ask for the gift of obedience and pray for those who suffer sorrow.

PERSONAL REFLECTIONS:

The Fourth Sorrowful Mystery

The Crucifixion

When they had crucified him, they divided up his clothes by casting lots. And sitting down, they kept watch over him there. Above his head they placed the written charge against him: THIS IS JESUS, THE KING OF THE JEWS. Two robbers were crucified with him, one on his right and one on his left. Those who passed by hurled insults at him, shaking their heads and saying, "You who are going to destroy the temple and build it in three days, save yourself! Come down from the cross, if you are the Son of God!" In the same way the chief priests, the teachers of the law and the elders mocked him. "He saved others," they said, "but he can't save himself! He's the King of Israel! Let him come down now from the cross, and we will believe in him. He trusts in God. Let God rescue him now if he wants him, for he said, 'I am the Son of God.' " In the same way the robbers who were crucified with him also heaped insults on him. From the sixth hour until the ninth hour darkness came over all the land. About the ninth hour Jesus cried out in a loud voice, "Eloi, Eloi, lama sabachthani?"—which means, "My God, my God, why have you forsaken me?" And when Jesus had cried out again in a loud voice, he gave up his spirit.

On the day of his Resurrection Jesus Christ left in the tomb the shroud which is the symbol of our infirmities, our weaknesses, our imperfections. Christ comes from the tomb triumphant—completely free of earthly limitation; He is animated with a life that is intense and perfect, and which vibrates in every fiber of his being. In him everything that is mortal has been absorbed by his glorified life. Here is the first element of the sanctity represented in the risen Christ: the elimination of everything that is corruptible, everything that is earthly and created; freedom from all defects, all infirmities, and all capacity for suffering. But there is also another element of sanctity: union with God, self- oblation and consecration to God. Only in heaven shall we be able to understand how completely Jesus lived for his Father during these blessed days. The life of the risen Christ became an infinite source of glory for his Father. Not a single effect of his sufferings was left in him, for now everything in him shone with brilliance and beauty and possessed strength and life; every atom of his being sang an unceasing canticle of praise. His holy humanity offered itself in a new manner to the glory of the Father.

PRAY

Our Father…

Lord Jesus Christ…

After completing the seven weeks beads say,

Glory be to the Father…

Ask for the gift of a holy death and pray for unity among Christians.

PERSONAL REFLECTIONS:

The First Glorious Mystery

The Resurrection

And when the Sabbath was past, Mary Magdalene, and Mary the mother of James, and Salome, bought spices, so that they might go and anoint him. And very early on the first day of the week they went to the tomb when the sun had risen. And they were saying to one another, "Who will roll away the stone for us from the door of the tomb?" And looking up, they saw that the stone was rolled back; -- it was very large. And entering the tomb, they saw a young man sitting on the right side, dressed in a white robe; and they were amazed. And he said to them, "Do not be amazed; you seek Jesus of Nazareth, who was crucified. He has risen, he is not here; see the place where they laid him. But go, tell his disciples and Peter that he is going before you to Galilee; there you will see him, as he told you."

Our Lord said to His Apostles before he departed from them: "If you loved me, you would indeed rejoice that I am going to the Father." To us also Christ repeats these words. If we love him, we shall rejoice in his glorification as we anticipate our own; we shall rejoice with Him that, after completing His course on earth, He ascends to the right hand of His Father, there to be exalted above all the heavens in infinite glory. But Jesus goes only to precede us; He does not separate himself from us, nor does he separate us from himself. If he enters into his glorious kingdom, it is to prepare a place for us there. He promises to return one day to take us with him so that, as he says, where he is we also may be. True, we are already there in the glory and happiness of Christ, by our title as his heirs; but we shall one day be there in reality. Has not Christ asked this of his Father? "Father, I will that where I am, they also whom Thou hast given me may be with Me." Let us then say to Christ Jesus: "Draw us into your triumphal march, O glorious and all-powerful Conqueror! Make us live in heaven by faith and hope and love. Help us to detach ourselves from the fleeting things of earth in order that we may seek the true and lasting goods of heaven!"

PRAY

Our Father…

Lord Jesus Christ…

After completing the seven weeks beads say,

Glory be to the Father…

Ask for the gift of fortitude and pray for the needs of your community.

PERSONAL REFLECTIONS:

The Second Glorious Mystery

The Ascension

After he said this, he was taken up before their very eyes, and a cloud hid him from their sight. They were looking intently up into the sky as he was going, when suddenly two men dressed in white stood beside them. "Men of Galilee," they said, "why do you stand here looking into the sky? This same Jesus, who has been taken from you into heaven, will come back in the same way you have seen him go into heaven."

The Holy Spirit appeared under the form of tongues of fire in order to fill the Disciples with Himself and to prepare them to bear witness to Jesus. He also came to fill their hearts with love.

He is the Person of Love in the life of God. He is also like a breath, being Spirit, an aspiration of infinite Love, from which we draw the breath of life. On the day of Pentecost the Divine Spirit communicated such an abundance of life to the whole Church that to symbolize it "there came a sound from heaven, as of a violent wind coming, and it filled the whole house where they were sitting." But it is also for us and to us that the Holy Spirit has come, for the group in the Cenacle represented the whole Church. The Holy Spirit came to remain with the Church forever. This is the promise of Jesus Himself. He dwells in the Church permanently and unfailingly, performing in it without ceasing, his action of life-giving and sanctification. He establishes the Church infallibly in the truth. It is he who makes the Church blossom forth with a marvelous supernatural fruitfulness, for he brings to life and full fruition in all believers those heroic virtues which are the marks of true sanctity. As God breathed life into the first man, so God the Holy Spirit breathes life into His church and continues to do so throughout the ages.

PRAY

Our Father…

Lord Jesus Christ…

After completing the seven weeks beads say,

Glory be to the Father…

Ask for gifts of the Holy Spirit and pray for the mission of the Church.

PERSONAL REFLECTIONS:

The Third Glorious Mystery

Pentecost

When the day of Pentecost came, they were all together in one place. Suddenly a sound like the blowing of a violent wind came from heaven and filled the whole house where they were sitting. They saw what seemed to be tongues of fire that separated and came to rest on each of them. All of them were filled with the Holy Spirit and began to speak in other tongues as the Spirit enabled them. Now there were staying in Jerusalem God-fearing Jews from every nation under heaven. When they heard this sound, a crowd came together in bewilderment, because each one heard them speaking in his own language. Utterly amazed, they asked: "Are not all these men who are speaking Galileans? Then how is it that each of us hears them in his own native language? Parthians, Medes and Elamites; residents of Mesopotamia, Judea and Cappadocia, Pontus and Asia, Phrygia and Pamphylia, Egypt and the parts of Libya near Cyrene; visitors from Rome (both Jews and converts to Judaism, Cretans and Arabs), we hear them declaring the wonders of God in our own tongues!"

Our Lord tells us in Revelation that to he who overcomes he will give to sit down with him on his throne, as he overcame and sat down on his Father's. St. Paul tells us in 1 Corinthians that if we run the race we too shall receive a heavenly crown, and St. John in Revelation sees the Blessed Mother as a woman clothed with the sun and on her head a crown of twelve stars. As a favored daughter of God the Father, the Spouse of God the Holy Spirit and the Mother of God the Son, we celebrate the ancient belief that the Blessed Mother of our Lord has indeed run the race and, like other saints of heaven, received her heavenly crown. In this we anticipate our own crowning one day, when we have run the race with God's help and are invited to the wedding feast of the Lamb, prepared as a bride for her Bridegroom. Scripture says that those who are of God are called gods, and St. Paul also tells us that we shall one day command angels. Think of it: Received into the arms of our Blessed Savior, escorted past the glorious heavenly hosts, filled with the brilliance of God the Holy Spirit and crowned by God Himself in light and in glory – what a day that shall be!

PRAY

Our Father…

Lord Jesus Christ…

After completing the seven weeks beads say,

Glory be to the Father…

Ask for the gift of holy hope and pray for the needs of all Christian people.

PERSONAL REFLECTIONS:

The Fourth Glorious Mystery
The Crowning

To him who overcomes, I will give the right to sit with me on my throne, just as I overcame and sat down with my Father on his throne. He who has an ear, let him hear what the Spirit says to the churches."

The Angelus

The Angel of the Lord declared unto Mary:

> And she conceived of the Holy Spirit.

Hail Mary, full of grace, the Lord is with thee; blessed art thou among women and blessed is the fruit of thy womb, Jesus. Holy Mary, Mother of God, pray for us sinners, now and at the hour of our death. Amen.

Behold the handmaid of the Lord:

> Be it done unto me according to Thy word.

Hail Mary, full of grace, the Lord is with thee; blessed art thou among women and blessed is the fruit of thy womb, Jesus. Holy Mary, Mother of God, pray for us sinners, now and at the hour of our death. Amen.

And the Word was made Flesh:

> And dwelt among us.

Hail Mary, full of grace, the Lord is with thee; blessed art thou among women and blessed is the fruit of thy womb, Jesus. Holy Mary, Mother of God, pray for us sinners, now and at the hour of our death. Amen.

Pray for us, O Holy Mother of God, that we may be made worthy of the promises of Christ.

Let us pray:

We beseech thee, O Lord, pour thy grace into our hearts; that as we have known the Incarnation of thy Son Jesus Christ by the message of an angel, so by his + cross and passion, we may be brought to the glory of his resurrection. We ask this through Christ our Lord.

Amen.

The Salve Regina [Hail Holy Queen]

Hail, Holy Queen, Mother of Mercy, our Life, our Sweetness, and our Hope!

To Thee do we cry, poor banished children of Eve. To Thee do we send up our sighs mourning and weeping in this valley of tears.

Turn then, most gracious Advocate, Thine Eyes of Mercy toward us, and after this our exile show us the Blessed Fruit of thy Womb, Jesus.

O clement, O loving, O sweet Virgin Mary: Pray for us O Holy Mother of God, that we may be made worthy of the promises of Christ.

Amen.

Made in the USA
San Bernardino, CA
03 November 2016